Cover art by Drew Kersey

ISBN: 0615850138

ISBN-13: 978-0615850139

This is a work of fiction. Names, characters, places, businesses and incidents are either the product of the author's imagination or are used fictitiously. Any resemblance to actual persons, living or dead, businesses, events or locales is purely coincidental.

For Nathan and Matthew
Do not open until Christmas

Spirit of Christmas

A NOVELLA BY

KYLE ANDREWS

Chapter One

The world was aglow with the dazzling lights and whimsical sounds of Christmas. Thousands of years of history and tradition, boiled down to their most basic elements and recreated year after year, to the delight of all who cared to take part. The feeling of the season was unmistakable. To a small boy like Aidan Shores, it was like spending a month-long vacation in Wonderland.

When Aidan was very small, he lived just outside of Dallas, Texas. There, Christmas could either be snowy and cold, or seventy degrees and sunny. People would decorate with inflatable snowmen in their front yards, while wearing short sleeves and flip-flops. He and his parents always had a good laugh about that.

For as long as he could remember, Aidan's father would tell him stories about Christmases when he was a kid himself, many, many years earlier.

Aidan would curl up on the couch with a freshly-baked sugar cookie and listen to his father tell stories of ice skating on a frozen pond and hiking through the snowy woods. As his father told these stories, he looked out the window, across the lush green lawn and even at a very young age, Aidan could tell that his father missed those Christmases.

The Shores family spent Aidan's first seven Christmases in Texas. For the first two of those, Aidan was the only child in the house, but he couldn't remember what those years were like. For as far back as he could remember, Aidan's little sister, Madison, had been there for the celebration.

She was okay. Aidan didn't mind having Madison around most of the time. She followed him around and did pretty much whatever he told her to do, which he enjoyed.

Their family was happy. Even though his parents missed their families—especially around Christmas—they managed to create their own traditions.

They would wake up early and open the presents that Santa had left for them. Then, they would spend the rest of the morning calling all of those family members who lived far away and telling them all about their new toys and games.

By noon, they would be visiting with friends and neighbors. By three o'clock, they would be asleep on the floor, amidst the piles of wrapping paper and empty boxes. By six, they would be stuffed full of all the food that they only seemed to eat around Christmas. By seven, they would be reading Christmas stories from a really fancy looking book that Aidan's mother kept packed away with the Christmas decorations.

And then, it was over.

For seven years, this was the Christmas that Aidan had known. Now, he was hardly to the point of being set in his ways after only seven years, but this was what he had come to expect. He never dreamed of being able to spend Christmas in that far away land where his parents had grown up—the place filled with snow and trees and frozen ponds. He didn't even know how to dream of such a place. Yet, this was where Aidan would spend his eighth Christmas. The faraway land, which had existed only in his imagination up until that year...

New Jersey.

Even the name of this wondrous place sounded shiny and exciting.

Sure, he'd seen New Jersey before, but that was when it was hot and people were swimming in the ocean. This was different. This was the place that his father had told him about each year, right along with Rudolph and Frosty.

Aidan could hardly believe it. His parents had seemed so upset in recent months. His father was spending more time at home than normal. His mother had spent more time crying than normal.

They yelled at each other, but then spent a lot of time hugging each other. He never would have imagined that his parents were planning such an amazing adventure.

It was shortly after Thanksgiving when his mother and father began putting everything they owned into boxes. At first, Aidan wondered why they were packing so many things for one trip, but his father eventually sat him down with Maddie and told them that they weren't going to be coming back to Texas after Christmas. They weren't just going to *visit* New Jersey, they were going to *live* there.

Aidan handled this information rather well. At first, he didn't think of the friends that he was leaving behind or the house that he would never see again. He didn't think about starting in a new school or meeting new kids. All he could think about was Christmas.

Madison, on the other hand, freaked out. When her father explained to her that she would have to leave her room and her house and her yard, Madison screamed. She did not want to go, and she insisted that she would stay behind.

When her father explained that new people would be living in their house, Madison threatened to stay and live with them. Her father didn't argue, which only made Madison more upset. She cried and ran up to her room, where her father went to find her.

Aidan was left alone. He could hear his mother in another room, taping up a box. He could hear Maddie crying and yelling at her father. He could hear his father begging her to calm down.

As he listened to all of these things, Aidan looked out the window, into the bright and sunny day, and dreamed of making snowmen.

Chapter Two

"Santa Claus will find us, right?" Aidan asked his mother, with as much urgency as an adult might ask whether or not the coffee pot was turned off before leaving the house.

"Santa will find us," his mother assured him. "I sent a change of address postcard to him last week."

After two weeks of packing, they were leaving the house, never to return; but this part of their journey hadn't yet sunken in for Aidan. All that he could think about was the road ahead. It wasn't until they were walking out the door that the mood suddenly changed.

"Madison, let's go!" his father yelled into the house, before turning to Aidan's mother and asking, "What's she doing in there?"

"She is kissing all of the light switches and outlets goodbye," his mother said with just a hint of a smile.

"Is that safe?" his dad replied.

His mother only shrugged.

As Aidan looked up at his mother, to share in the craziness of his little sister and laugh at her silliness, he noticed that his mother wasn't exactly happy. Though she smiled, she was looking into the house as though she was about to cry.

His father put an arm around her and held her close as he said, "This is a good thing."

"Are you sure?" she asked, wiping a tear from her cheek.

Aidan looked up at his mother and smiled as wide as he could as he said, "This is a *really* good thing, Mom."

Aidan looked into the house, just as Maddie was walking out. Behind her, the place was empty. None of their furniture remained. None of their toys. No food. No clothes. Everything that they owned was on a truck, making its way across the country, and his parents had forbidden Aidan from riding along with those things.

In that moment, the house no longer seemed like home to Aidan. It seemed like a place he'd *once* lived—though, of course, he couldn't quite pinpoint what that feeling was or what it meant.

His father locked the front door as the family walked down the driveway, toward their car. To Aidan, it seemed like his neighbors should be outside, waving goodbye and making a big deal of the situation, but none of them were outside. As his family drove away from the place they'd once lived, Aidan saw no familiar faces watching them go.

"Look at that," his mother said to his father, in a quiet voice which meant that they were having a grownup conversation. "The Pierces are selling their house."

"I want to go home!" Maddie screamed, bursting into tears beside Aidan.

"We can't go back, sweetie. This road only goes forward," his father replied.

"I want to go back! Please!" Maddie screamed, now sobbing uncontrollably.

Aidan's parents looked at each other, but didn't say anything. Instead, his mother turned and looked out the window and his daddy reached over and took his wife's hand.

Aidan looked over to Maddie, whose face was bright red and wet with tears. He smiled at her and said, "There's snow in New Jersey, Maddie."

"I don't care!" Madison screamed.

"That means we have to drink extra hot chocolate."

"I don't care!"

Aidan took a deep breath, trying to think of some way to cheer up his little sister. All he could think to do was reach over and take her hand.

∞

He thought that she would cry until they reached New Jersey, two days later. Luckily, she fell asleep a few hours into their drive and when she woke up, Madison seemed to be handling the situation much better. After that, her fits and outbursts came in waves. For as long as Aidan and his parents could keep her mind off of the fact that they were leaving their home, she was fine. If she remembered, chaos ensued.

Aidan could feel change coming. He had no idea what to expect when he got to New Jersey; no idea what his life would be like. As they drove, he thought more and more about all of the things that he was leaving behind and he felt his stomach churning, but he was not one for screaming and crying. When Aidan was nervous, he stayed quiet, so *quiet* was how he spent most of their drive.

Miles of highway passed by his window and Aidan watched as green grass and sunshine turned to gray skies and rain. Flat land turned to hills and then to mountains. By the time they passed through Tennessee, snow was falling.

His mother and father had run out of conversation and had been quiet for hours. Christmas music was playing on the car's radio. Maddie was playing a video game on her mother's cell phone. The car was calm, which only made the situation feel stranger to Aidan. *There should be more to this life-changing drive than Christmas music and peace*, he thought, though not in those exact words.

The world seemed different to him. While he knew why things looked different outside of his window, he couldn't figure out why things *felt* different. Even within the car, colors seemed somehow changed.

Aidan's eyes wandered from the window, to the rear-view mirror, where they caught his father's eyes looking back at him. His father looked from the mirror, to the road, and then back. He said nothing to Aidan. He just watched, as though to see how his son was feeling.

Aidan knew that his father was sensing his uneasiness and he could have chosen to fuss about it, but he didn't. Instead, Aidan looked back to his father and smiled.

His father winked back.

Aidan then looked to the mirror on the side of the car, next to his mother's window. In that mirror, he could see his mother's reflection as she looked out the window, into the world that passed them by. She didn't notice Aidan watching her.

"You know what they have in New Jersey that we never had in Texas?" Aidan's father asked, breaking the silence amongst the family.

Aidan looked back to him and asked, "What?"

"*Real* Christmas trees."

"Rich Foster has a real Christmas tree in his house. I saw it last week," Aidan replied.

"Well, *we* never had one. It's too warm in Texas, so they dry out and die way before Christmas. But in New Jersey, it's not as hot, so they live longer. Which means, we can get one," his father told him.

Aidan and Maddie grinned from ear to ear when they heard this news. Their mother, on the other hand, looked to her husband without seeming very happy at all.

"Is it cold inside, in New Jersey?" Maddie asked her father.

"No, it's not cold. We have heaters up there. And fireplaces, which we can sit next to and drink hot chocolate," their father told her.

Maddie took a moment to think about her response, and then asked, "But if it's not cold *inside*, how do the trees live longer?"

Up front, their mother and father looked at each other and then started laughing. They laughed so hard that Aidan couldn't help but join them, and then Maddie.

After a few moments of laughing together, Maddie stopped and looked to her brother and said, "I'm serious."

This only made their parents laugh harder. Neither Aidan nor Maddie had any idea why they were laughing, but they enjoyed it nonetheless.

Chapter Three

Usually, when Aidan saw New Jersey, it was summertime. The beaches were filled with people; many of whom were very tan and wore a lot of gold jewelry. The shops along the boardwalk were always open for business. There were fairs and arcades.

New Jersey in the wintertime was something else entirely. For starters, the beaches were empty. The water, which usually looked so inviting, now took on a different tone. He could tell that it was cold, just by looking at it. The sand seemed more gray than normal. The shops were closed and many of them were boarded up. When they passed by boardwalks which usually had rides and games, there was nothing to see. Even the rides had been boarded up for the winter.

Moving away from the beach was another story. These areas were normally not the liveliest. Down those roads, there were houses which looked as though they had been there since the birth of Santa Claus himself. Aidan had only ever seen such houses on old TV shows, which his mother and father told him were around even before *they* were born, so they must have been really old.

These houses were decorated for Christmas, and even though it was daytime and there were no Christmas lights shining, the houses were beautiful. There was garland made from the pine tree trimmings and red bows. There were silver bells on lampposts and an impressive sleigh, with wooden reindeer and a sculpture of Santa Claus in the driver's seat. Aidan had no idea where the owners of that house kept those decorations for the rest of the year, but he was captivated by them.

At the end of that street, there was a large and somewhat scary church which had a nativity scene in front. Aidan had seen nativity scenes before, but it was somehow different seeing it surrounded by snow.

Everywhere he looked, there were people bundled in their heaviest winter coats, with gloves, hats and scarves. They looked like the tiny figurines that went along with the porcelain Christmas village that his mother put out every year.

"Look!" Maddie yelled as she pressed her hand against the window on her side of the car.

When Aidan turned, he saw a park which had a pond in the center. The pond was frozen over, allowing people to ice skate over it. Aidan's jaw dropped when he saw this. It was just like in the stories that his father had told him.

"Won't they fall into the water?" he asked his parents, never taking his eyes off of the skaters.

"Not if they're lucky," his mother replied.

"I fell in the water once," his father added. "Which is a good reason to never be the first one out there."

They continued to drive past the park, and Aidan kept his eyes on the skaters, half-expecting one of them to vanish beneath the water at any moment. None of them did.

As they went, they passed the town library, the elementary school and a very interesting-looking ice cream shop that Aidan hoped to explore further in the future. They then turned down a residential street and followed it to another. All along the way, there were houses with Christmas decorations that seemed more magical than those that people put up in Texas—though they probably all came from the same mega-chain retailer that had stores all over the country.

The closer they got to his grandmother's house, the more Aidan wanted to hop out of the car and take a deep breath of the crisp winter air. At the same time, his mother seemed to grow quieter and more distant. Aidan could always tell when she was upset about something, and while she didn't seem *angry*, she certainly seemed upset in some way.

Grandma's house was old. Aidan's father once told him that the house had been around since before people drove cars. Aidan wasn't sure whether or not Grandma had lived there that entire time, but he imagined that she had. She was, after all, the oldest person that Aidan knew.

The house sat at the top of a small hill. It had a large porch in front and such curves and peaks that Aidan couldn't help but think that it looked like a freshly-made gingerbread house. Even without decorations, it fit in perfectly with the season.

As the car came to a stop and everyone rushed to get out, the warmth of the car's heater was replaced by the brisk winter air, scented with the essence of fires burning in several nearby homes. Where Aidan came from, they rarely lit fires in their fireplace, which was far too small for a stack of logs. Instead, they had porcelain logs and gas which kept the fire going. It didn't smell very nice at all.

He wanted cocoa, and a sled, and to build a snowman, and about a hundred other things which flooded his mind as he entered this strange new world.

Maddie, on the other hand, was clinging to her mother's side, looking up at the big house as though it were looking back.

"Are there ghosts?" Maddie asked her mother.

Aidan's mother rubbed Maddie's back and asked, "What do you know about ghosts?"

"Aidan says that they're invisible and come into your room at night and watch you sleep," Maddie told her mother, who immediately looked at Aidan with eyes that scared him more than any ghost ever could have.

"That's for Halloween, stupid," Aidan said to Maddie, hoping to set her mind at ease and prevent himself from being punished for scaring his sister.

Aidan's father stood outside of the house, looking up at it. Aidan walked to his side and looked up as well, though he wasn't quite sure what they were looking at.

"I come back here, and I'm your age again," his father told him. "Seems like yesterday."

"Only we have computers now," Aidan smiled.

"We had computers. They were just about as powerful as the chip that makes your shoes blink when you walk, but we had them and we thought they were the coolest things ever," his father explained, with a grin on his face. "Of course, we also played outside and used our imaginations. You kids today have no respect for the power of a good imagination."

"You did not just say 'you kids today,'" Aidan's mother said to her husband as she walked up beside him, carrying Maddie in her arms.

"Whippersnappers," his father replied. "Hooligans. The whole lot of 'em."

Aidan had no idea what these words meant, but the way his father said them made him smile.

The front door of the house opened, and Aidan's Grandma walked onto the porch, pulling a sweater around her as she went. She stood at the top of the porch steps and looked at her son and his family for a moment before asking, "Well, do you plan on spending the winter out there or do you want to come in?"

Aidan's mother lowered Maddie onto the ground and the two children ran to greet Grandma. Their parents stayed behind for just a second or two before following. As they walked up to the house, Aidan's father put his arm around his mother and kissed her on the head. Aidan saw this as he climbed the porch steps. He liked it when they weren't fighting.

The strange part was that his parents weren't smiling. They didn't seem happy to be at that house at all. While Aidan was excited to see his grandmother and to spend Christmas in New Jersey, seeing his parents at that particular moment made him feel a sense of unexplainable sadness.

"I hope you like hamburgers," Grandma said as Aidan hurried into her arms and gave her a big hug.

Maddie was right beside Aidan and replied, "I love hamboogers."

"Do you like French fries?" Grandma asked.

Maddie nodded.

"Do you like milkshakes?"

Another nod.

"Do you like onion rings?"

This one puzzled Maddie, who asked, "What's an onion ring?"

Grandma looked past the children, to her son, and said, "They don't know what onion rings are? Honestly, I think you're raising your children all wrong."

"We also lock them in closets and give them alcohol so they'll fall asleep," his father replied; without a smile, but Aidan could tell that he was joking.

"Yeah, yeah. That's fine. Whatever. But honestly, no onion rings?"

As their parents climbed the porch steps, the children moved to allow them to hug Grandma.

"Hello, Mom," his father said, now with a smile, as he gave his mother a hug. "Are you sure about this?"

"I'm sure," Grandma whispered back, moving to hug Aidan's mother. "Now, if your sister and her husband ever moved in, I might have a problem. That boy is... so special."

As Aidan's mother hugged Grandma, Aidan heard her whisper, "Thank you."

Once again, there came a sense of unhappiness. Aidan couldn't explain it. He loved his Grandma, and he thought that spending Christmas there would be the most amazing thing ever—topping the previous holder of the title, which was watching the Thanksgiving parade on TV. Despite all of that excitement, there was something darker just beneath the surface. The world was taking an unexpected turn and nobody was telling him what it was that he should be worried about.

Chapter Four

Grandma's house was not like the house that Aidan had lived in, back in Texas. His old house had wood floors, but the wood floors in Grandma's house looked older. There was a rug that covered a section of the floor in the family room. It was red, with all sorts of fancy swirls and swooshes of color, which had been worn over many years. Just looking at that rug made Aidan think that the house was really old.

The walls were painted a light brown color, with white trim. It looked so clean and fresh that Aidan was afraid to touch anything, but he knew that Maddie would be sure to make a mess of things in no time. She had a habit of getting marker ink on walls, even if she didn't mean to do it.

The last time Aidan visited Grandma, the summer before last, her old furniture had white fabric on it, with yellow designs sewn in. The seats were worn and dirty. Now, the furniture was the same, but the fabric which covered them was different. The new fabric was red, with brown designs. It fit in well with the few Christmas decorations that Grandma had scattered around the house.

"Dad says we can get a real tree," Aidan said to Grandma, as he sat in the family room with her after dinner. His father was cleaning dishes in the kitchen, while his mother was getting Maddie changed into her pajamas upstairs.

"I always get a real tree," Grandma replied. "Of course, I haven't been able to decorate it very well for a few years now. I'm getting old, you know."

"Mom says that when an old person says that, they want you to tell them that they're not old," Aidan replied.

Grandma nodded just slightly and smiled, "That's true."

Aidan smiled and said, "You're not old, Grandma."

"You're a sweet boy. You're growing up so fast too. Are you driving yet?"

"No! I'm only eight."

"Really? Do you have a job?"

"I'm eight!"

"Do you have... a mortgage?"

"What's a—umm..."

"Mortgage?" Grandma asked, and Aidan nodded. "It's when the bank helps you pay for a house, and then you pay them back a little bit each month."

"Oh," Aidan understood. "I think Mom and Dad had one of those back in Texas."

Grandma smiled, but that same sense of looming darkness washed across her face. She put an arm around him and walked with him to the fireplace, which had no fire burning in it. There, she sat on the hearth and looked Aidan in the eyes as she asked, "What do you love more than anything in the whole world?"

Aidan shrugged. He didn't know what she wanted him to say.

"Do you love your sister?" Grandma asked.

Aidan scrunched his nose in disgust and said, "I guess so."

Grandma smiled at that. She said, "Of course you do. And do you love your Mommy and Daddy?"

Aidan nodded.

"Do you love them more than your toys?"

Aidan thought about that for a second or two and reluctantly nodded. Again, Grandma smiled.

"Do you love them more than cookies and ice cream?"

Aidan nodded once more.

"And more than your old house in Texas?"

This time, when Aidan nodded, he felt that darkness, hidden inside of her question. Only this time, when Grandma smiled, that darkness seemed less scary.

"I don't miss my old house," Aidan told her.

"You don't?"

Aidan shook his head.

"Why not?"

Aidan shrugged at this question.

"Can I tell you a secret?" Grandma asked.

Aidan nodded.

Leaning in close, Grandma whispered to Aidan, "I've missed my home for a very long time."

"But you always lived here."

Grandma smiled and said, "That's true."

∞

That night, Aidan slept in his new room for the first time. It was the same room that his father had slept in as a child, and if Aidan looked inside the closet, next to the door, near the baseboard, he could see where his father had signed his name with a pencil, when he was not much older than Aidan.

The room hadn't been used for many years. It had a bed and a dresser, but all of his father's things had been packed up long ago.

Soon, Aidan's things would arrive on the truck and he would make the room his own. On that night, however, he enjoyed the emptiness. To him it felt like an adventure, spent in a wide open place, sleeping beneath the moonlight.

It wasn't *actually* moonlight. There were thick clouds in the sky, preventing the moonlight from shining down. Instead, Aidan's room was aglow with blinking lights of various colors, which came from the Christmas decorations on nearby houses.

He tried to resist the urge to get out of bed. He knew that his parents wanted him to go to sleep and if they heard him walking around, they would get upset. However, he saw those lights blinking on his walls and ceiling and he imagined what the street must look like. While the image in his head was mighty impressive, he couldn't stop himself from looking out at the real thing.

Standing at his window, Aidan could see houses to the left and right, which seemed to stretch into eternity. Some were lined with Christmas lights and inflatable snowmen, which he had seen back in Texas as well. Others had fewer lights, but he could see fake candles in the windows and bows on every porch light. There were wreaths and garland. Many houses had stars hanging at their highest point, shining brighter than any of their other decorations. There was one lawn which had a wooden gingerbread house in front, complete with gingerbread people.

Another lawn had a group of mannequins, dressed like carolers. Aidan could all but hear their music.

If he looked over the roofs of the houses in front of him, Aidan could see the houses on the next street and beyond, most with similar decorations.

The sight took his breath away. He stood at the window with his mouth hanging open and his nose pressed against the glass. With each exhale, the world was filled with fog and every light was given a halo.

Aidan's eyes shifted back to the house directly across the street from him. In the highest window of that house, lit only by a fake candle which colored everything around it orange, Aidan spotted a figure. At first, he could barely see the form. Compared to most windows on the street, the window across from him was darkly lit, so Aidan's eyes needed time to find their focus on that figure.

The thing that stood out the most was the smile. It was wider than any normal smile that he had ever seen. The more he stared at it, the more unnerving the smile became. Aidan started to feel as though the smile was being directed at him, and this idea sent a chill up his spine.

Next, he saw the hand. Covered with a mitten, the hand was held high, as though it was waving at him—but it never moved.

The eyes were dark; hidden by the shadows which were cast by the orange light of the fake candle.

The beard was long and white. The hat was red.

It was at this point that Aidan realized that he was looking at Santa Claus—or a decoration made in his image.

He chuckled at himself, thinking how stupid he was for being scared of Santa. It was so silly and strange, and anyone who heard about it would definitely think that he was a scaredy-cat.

There had to have been a hundred different Santas scattered around that street. Some were waving. Others were riding in a sleigh. A couple of them were climbing down chimneys—and one seemed to be stuck with his legs hanging out.

Looking at them all reminded Aidan that Santa really was coming. Soon, he would be delivering presents and stuffing stockings full of candy.

Aidan ran back to his bed and hurried to pull the covers over his head. He wanted to get to sleep as quickly as possible, because every new day brought him closer to Santa's arrival.

Chapter Five

Aidan was not very close with his cousins, Sarah and Max. They were the children of his father's brother, Michael, and Aidan had only met them a few times in his entire life. Sure, his father spoke with Uncle Michael on the phone very often, and Aidan's mother was even close friends with Michael's wife, Jessica. However, up until they moved back to New Jersey, the family had rarely gathered and the kids never spoke with each other.

Sarah was four years older than Aidan. Being the mature twelve-year-old that she was, she wanted very little to do with the kids and their silly games. So, Aidan and Maddie spent most of their time with Max when their parents took them to Uncle Michael's house, two days after they arrived in New Jersey.

Max was very different than his sister. While she preferred to be by herself and keep things proper and tidy, Max seemed just a little bit wild. He enjoyed running around and leaving his toys wherever they happened to fall. He also spoke with Aidan and

Maddie as though they had been best friends for years, rather than cousins who barely knew each other.

As they ate their lunch at the kitchen table, their mothers sat in the living room, talking amongst themselves. They would laugh in bursts, and then get really quiet. Aidan watched as his aunt put her hand on his mother's arm and shook her head.

He had become an expert at watching the adults in his life talk when they didn't think he was watching. When they didn't think he was paying any attention, they would say things that they normally wouldn't say in front of him. Most of the time, the adults were either too far away for him to hear, or they would say things that he didn't understand. This frustrated Aidan, because he was old enough to recognize when his mother wasn't happy. He knew that she was sad, because she always got quiet and crossed her arms over her chest when she was sad.

The more interesting thing was that Aidan saw something in his mother's eyes that he normally didn't see in her or his father. It was a look that he regularly only saw in Maddie's eyes, when she was convinced that there was a monster under her bed or in her closet.

"Aidan?" Max said, poking Aidan's arm with his finger. "A-A-A-A-Aidan? What are you looking at?"

"He's looking at Mommy," Maddie replied.

"I know he's looking at Mommy," Max told her. "But she's not *your* Mommy."

"She is too my Mommy!"

"No, she's *my* Mommy!"

"No!" Maddie yelled, throwing her head back dramatically. "I'm talking about *my* Mommy."

Max seemed to finally catch on as he said, "Oh. Why didn't you say that you were talking about *your* Mommy?"

Maddie just shrugged in response. Aidan turned back to his grilled cheese and took a mouthful. He looked to Max, who smiled at him, revealing teeth which were covered with half-chewed food.

Max quickly swallowed and asked, "How will Santa know that you're not in Texas anymore?"

"Mommy told him that we moved," Aidan replied.

"*Your* Mommy?"

Aidan rolled his eyes and replied, "Yes. *My* Mommy."

Max nodded and took a sip of his milk before saying, "That's good. Because this Christmas is going to be so, so, so cool. I'm getting night vision goggles."

"What are night vision goggles?" Maddie asked.

"They make everything look green," Max told her. "They're so, so, so cool."

"Well, I'm getting a fairy princess costume and ballet slippers. And a cell phone, with a data plane," Maddie smiled, "so it can fly. Fwoom!"

"I'm getting a cell phone too!" Max replied.

"I'm getting a tent and a sleeping bag," Aidan told Max. "And a flashlight."

"I'm getting a tent and a sleeping bag too!" Max grinned. "I already have a flashlight."

Max reached into his pocket and pulled out a little plastic clown. When he squeezed it, the clown's nose lit up.

Maddie seemed very impressed with his clown flashlight. All she could manage to say was "Ooooh."

"I mean a *real* flashlight," Aidan told him. "The kind that the police use when they break into peoples' houses."

"Oh," Max nodded, now understanding what Aidan was saying. He quickly added, "I'm getting one of those too."

"Me too!" Maddie yelled.

Aidan put his hand on his sister's shoulder and sadly informed her, "Nuh-uh. You're a girl. Girls can't be policemen."

Maddie grew upset, saying, "Can too."

"Can not."

"Can too."

"Can not."

"Then what can a girl be?" Maddie asked, genuinely puzzled.

Aidan shrugged and told her, "I heard Dad say that women were like werewolves."

"What's werewolves?"

Aidan shrugged again.

"Mommy!" Maddie suddenly yelled, causing both boys to jump back in their seats.

From the other room, Aidan and Maddie's mother replied, "What?"

"What's werewolves?!" Maddie yelled.

"They're like doggies, sweetie," their mother yelled back.

"Really big doggies," Aunt Jessica added.

"Why would Daddy say that women are like big doggies?!"

There was a pause before their mother replied, saying, "Because Daddy doesn't know what's good for him, sweetie."

"Thank you, Mommy!"

"You're welcome, sweetie."

From the other room, Aidan heard his mother and his aunt begin laughing. He didn't know why they were laughing, but he couldn't help but smile. He was happy that his mother was happy.

When Max saw Aidan smile, he smiled too. When Maddie saw Max smile, she smiled.

∞

Lunchtime was the calm before the storm. After the kids were done eating, they left the table and headed straight for the toys. They started by pulling out toy cars and racing them around the basement.

After several laps around the basement, Aidan ran his car up the side of a chair as though it was a ramp. He held that car as high as he could, pretending that it was flying through the air in slow motion, while Max and Maddie watched in awe.

Max quickly insisted that his car could fly higher and farther than Aidan's.

The competition quickly led to cars being thrown across the basement and crashing into the wall. Both mothers yelled at the kids from upstairs and ordered them to find something quieter to play with.

Mothers always seemed to know how to ruin a perfectly good day. Aidan didn't think that they were harming anything by playing with their toys. Why were they given toys in the first place, if all their mothers were ever going to do was yell at them for playing? It made no sense.

As much as he would have liked to protest, he chose not to. He rarely fussed or fought with his parents, since Maddie was so much better at it than he was. Instead, he sat in the basement with Max and Maddie and watched them brood.

"Mommy's so stupid," Max fussed, crossing his arms. "I hate her."

"I don't hate *my* Mommy," Maddie replied, with a tone that was equally fussy and with an upset look on her face.

"I just want to play," Max argued.

Maddie nodded, "I just want to play too."

As he watched Maddie and Max, Aidan came to realize that he was the oldest person in the room. He was the one who needed to be in charge and keep the kids in line. This also meant that he could probably get them to play whatever *he* wanted to play.

"Hide and seek!" Aidan smiled.

"Yeah!" Maddie yelled. A look of such excitement filled her face that she looked as though she had just won a trip to Disneyland.

"I don't like hide and seek," Max protested. "I never get to seek. I always hide. And nobody ever finds me."

"You want to find us?" Aidan asked.

"It's my house. You'll never be able to hide from me," Max said, with a sigh.

"Will too!" Aidan argued.

"Will too!" Maddie repeated.

The game was on. Max vowed that he would be able to find Aidan and Maddie, no matter where they hid, but Aidan laughed in the face of his opponent. This resulted in Max commenting that Aidan's breath smelled like grilled cheese.

After a good laugh, Max stood against the wall. His eyes were covered as he began to count.

Maddie ran as fast as she could, frantically looking for a place to hide. She looked under tables and behind chairs. Aidan didn't see where she eventually chose to hide, because while she was running around and making a lot of noise, Aidan quietly crept up the stairs.

His mother and his aunt were in the kitchen, cleaning dishes. They were talking, but in a quiet tone that made it impossible for Aidan to hear what they were saying.

He walked to the family room and scanned it for someplace where he might hide. He looked for boxes that would be large enough for him to fit in. He looked for hard to reach corners. In the end, the family room would not be good enough.

In his head, Aidan was keeping count with Max. He knew that at any moment, Max would come running up the stairs and if he didn't find a hiding spot soon, Aidan would lose the game. He needed to think fast.

Turning in every direction, Aidan quickly looked all around the house—or as far as he could see while standing in the foyer. The kitchen wouldn't do, because he couldn't trust his aunt to keep his secret if Max were to ask her.

Going upstairs would require more time than he had to spare. He needed a spot and he needed it now!

He then saw a door under the stairs which led to the second floor. It was across from the door which led to the basement, so hiding in there was a risk, but it was the best chance that Aidan had. He hurried to the door and opened it, finding a closet inside. He hurried into the closet and closed the door behind him.

Simply standing in the closet wouldn't be enough. He lowered himself to the floor and squeezed his way behind a vacuum cleaner and then a box, hiding in the darkest corner of the closet that he could possibly find.

Once settled, Aidan let out a sigh of relief. Downstairs, he could hear Maddie screaming. She had been found. Surely, Max would be coming for him next. With this in mind, Aidan pushed himself just a little bit deeper into the corner, and this was when he felt something move beside him. It felt like the wall itself had shifted, as though it were a door that was opening into some hidden room.

Of course, a hidden room would make for a way better hiding spot, so Aidan pushed his way into that tiny little room. As he crawled, he felt something brush against his face. It felt like a spider web at first, which caused Aidan to swat at it. As he did this, he realized that he was swatting a string, which was connected to something above him—a light.

He pulled on the string and light went on above him. Suddenly, Aidan found himself in a very small storage area, hidden behind the closet. In this storage area, he found stacks of Christmas presents, all wrapped and ready to be placed beneath the Christmas tree.

His mouth fell open. He had no idea what he was looking at. Why would Santa need to keep presents hidden in his uncle's house? Did his aunt and uncle know about this? Surely, his cousins didn't.

Should he tell? Should he scream? Should he open something?

Unable to wrap his mind around what he had found, Aidan chose to do none of those things. Instead, he turned off the light and left that storage area, closing the hidden door behind him. He sat in the closet, silent and stunned until Max threw open the door.

"Got you! I found you! I win! Ha-ha-ha!" Max cheered.

Somehow, the game didn't seem all that important anymore.

Chapter Six

Though Aidan wanted to forget what he had seen and pretend that it never happened, he could not get the image out of his mind. He thought of showing Maddie and Max, but as soon as the thought occurred to him, he imagined Maddie screaming and running to her mother. Questions would be asked. Grownups normally didn't like it when kids got into the areas where they weren't supposed to be.

He kept the secret to himself and it weighed heavily on him for the rest of the day.

By the time he returned to Grandma's house that evening, the moving truck had come and gone. What wasn't packed away in storage was now sitting in boxes, waiting to be unpacked.

Aidan found it strange, seeing all of the things that had once filled his old house, now scattered around Grandma's house. The place no longer felt like it was his grandmother's domain, but it also didn't feel like home.

He was silent at dinner that night. Grandma had a casserole waiting in the oven by the time he got back, and they were eating dinner by five o'clock. Maddie went on and on about her aunt and her cousins. She thought that Sarah was so cool because she was older and didn't have time to hang around with kids.

Grandma listened to Maddie and asked her many questions about Sarah and Max. Aidan thought it was strange, since Grandma lived so close to them and must have seen them all the time. Finally, he decided that Grandma was just being nice to Maddie, pretending to be interested.

At the other end of the table, Aidan's parents were talking to each other. They spoke in that quiet tone that they often used when they didn't want Aidan or Maddie to hear what they were saying. Aidan was proud of the fact that he could normally hear what they said anyway, despite the super-secret adult voices. The only problem was, he rarely understood the super-secret adult words, like *application* and *foreclose*.

As they spoke at dinner, Aidan wasn't even trying to listen. All he could think about was what he had seen. He needed answers.

"Where does Santa keep his presents?" he asked his parents, causing them to drop their conversation and look at him.

"Where does he keep his presents?" his father repeated, before shrugging and saying "I don't know. I guess he keeps them in his workshop until Christmas Eve, and then he loads them into his bag."

"How does he fit all of them into his bag?" Aidan asked.

"I don't know. Maybe it's a magic bag," his father told him.

This didn't help Aidan. He went on, asking, "But does he ever get them from somewhere else?"

"Like the store?" his mother asked.

Aidan nodded.

"I don't know. I guess he might," she said.

"But does he keep all of those presents in his workshop, even if he gets some of them in a store?"

"I don't know," his mother answered.

Cutting in, his father said, "Listen, buddy... Santa is magical. He doesn't need stores. He just kinda gets whatever presents he needs."

"But—"

"Sweetie, Santa doesn't like it when people start asking too many questions. Remember last year, when those really mean people tried to get Santa kicked out of the mall because they thought he was breaking the law?" Aidan's mother asked. "Santa didn't like that too much, did he?"

As they spoke to him, Aidan saw a look in their eyes. He hadn't seen this look since the time he accidentally turned on the wrong channel really late at night and found a show about people wrestling. Of course, he knew why they seemed nervous about him seeing that show on TV; they disliked him watching shows that were very violent. Now, he couldn't figure out why they had that look. It didn't make sense.

Just as he was about to ask another question, Maddie threw a forkful of her casserole on the floor and started laughing. Her parents quickly turned their attention to her and began yelling.

Aidan's question hadn't been answered. He still didn't know why there would be presents hidden in his uncle's house. Unfortunately, he wasn't very likely to get answers while his parents were yelling at Maddie.

∞

Aidan kept his questions to himself that night, as the family shopped for a Christmas tree. He tried to put those questions out of his mind, but it seemed like the more he tried, the more he needed to know.

Grandma was walking with Aidan and Maddie through the tent where the trees were being sold. His mother and father were there as well, but had wandered off by themselves.

Overhead, Christmas music was being played. As Aidan browsed through the forest of Christmas trees, he listened to

Santa Claus is Coming to Town. The song explained everything there was to know about Santa Claus, aside from why he would need to keep presents in someone's house.

"This one's nice. It's big and fat," Grandma said. "Just like you-know-who."

"Who?" Maddie asked.

Grandma raised her eyebrows and said, "Santa Claus. If we put a hat on this tree, I don't think we'd be able to tell the difference. Do you?"

"It's a tree!" Maddie replied.

"How does Santa see you when you're sleeping?" Aidan asked, having just heard that portion of the song on the speakers.

"He's magic," Grandma replied.

"What's magic?" Maddie asked.

"Santa Claus is magic."

Maddie shook her head, "No. What *is* magic?"

"Oh!" Grandma nodded. Aidan listened to her explanation of what magic was. She said, "Magic is when someone can do things that normal people can't do. They can turn pumpkins into stagecoaches. Or... Make mice into men."

"Like *Cinderella*?" Maddie asked.

"Yes. Her fairy godmother was magical. Just like Santa."

Aidan was more puzzled than ever. He asked, "Would Cinderella's fairy godmother need to keep a stagecoach at a person's house, so she could get it when she needed to change the pumpkin into a stagecoach?"

Grandma thought about his question for a moment, trying to make sense of it. After a few seconds, she said, "I... Don't think so."

She then turned and started looking at trees again. It seemed like every time Aidan asked a question about Santa, people started doing something else. Nobody wanted to talk about how Santa did what he did, and Aidan was beginning to wonder why.

As he continued to walk and look at trees, he rounded a corner and found his mother and father walking toward him. They seemed to be upset, which had become a common occurrence. Before they reached the rest of the family, Aidan heard his mother say, "I'm scared. I'm just really scared right now."

His father put an arm around his mother as they walked up to the kids and smiled.

"Find a good one yet?" his father asked.

"I like them all," Grandma replied. "But I think my favorite was back toward the front. How 'bout you kids?"

"I like the fat one!" Maddie laughed, picking up a pinecone that had fallen on the ground.

Aidan shrugged and said, "I like them all."

His father swooped in and picked Aidan up. He held him in his arms, just like he used to do when Aidan was a kid, and said, "Well, we have to pick one, kiddo. Let's hurry up, okay?"

Aidan's father hugged Aidan and kissed his head before setting him back on the ground once more. When he did, Aidan wiped the kiss off of his head and said, "Gross."

"Gross?!" his father replied. He turned to Aidan's mother and said, "He's growing up."

"How do you like it?" Grandma replied, with a smile.

Aidan's father walked over to Grandma and gave her a hug and a kiss on the head, saying, "I love you, Mommy."

"Gross!" Grandma yelled.

Right then, the mood seemed to change. Aidan couldn't help but laugh, and Maddie soon followed his lead. Soon, the whole family was smiling.

It was a good night.

Chapter Seven

Over the next several days, Aidan was caught in a frenzy of Christmas cheer. They decorated Grandma's house until it looked like Santa's workshop. Aidan and Maddie baked cookies with Grandma and delivered them to the local firehouse. Aidan thought that this was extra cool, because he got to see the fire truck up close. That had only happened once before, and he wasn't able to enjoy it then because his parents were yelling at him at the time.

He had watched most of his normal Christmas movies, and a few that Grandma had recorded on some outdated device that used some sort of tape to record. Aidan thought these tape things would be sticky, like most tape, but they weren't.

His mother and father weren't home for some of those festivities. They didn't go out together, but each of them would be out for hours at a time while Grandma was left to watch Aidan and his sister.

When Grandma decided that she needed to go to the mall and do some shopping before continuing with the Christmas baking, Maddie was excited. She knew who was at the mall around Christmas—at least back in Texas. Aidan knew as well, but as soon as the thought of Santa Claus crossed his mind, the questions returned.

Maddie was eager to talk to Santa. She wanted to make sure that he had gotten their new address and she wanted to update her Christmas list. Now, she wanted a tent and a flashlight, as well as a pony and a princess gown.

Grandma tried to tell Maddie that Santa's elves couldn't possibly make a live pony, but Maddie would not listen to this logic. She insisted that Santa was magical and he could pull a pony out of his bag if he really wanted to.

"But where will you put the pony?" Grandma asked, opening the car door in the mall's parking lot and helping Maddie out of her booster seat. Aidan was already climbing out of the car on his own.

"I'll keep her in my room and I can ride her every night before I go to bed," Maddie told Grandma with a laugh.

"Do you know what pony feet would do to my hardwood?" Grandma replied, hands on hips. "And ponies don't use potties. Do you really want to clean up that mess?"

"No!" Maddie laughed. "It's a maaaaaagic pony. Magic ponies don't poop."

"Magic ponies don't poop, huh?" Grandma continued as she held Maddie's hand and walked across the parking lot.

Aidan was too old to be holding his Grandma's hand when he walked, but she made sure that he stayed close by keeping a hand on his shoulder.

While Maddie and Grandma continued to talk about pony poop, Aidan walked through gray slush and listened to it crunch beneath his feet. He had Santa on the brain. If there would ever be a good time for him to ask Santa what was going on, this would be it—though Grandma was insisting that they wait for their parents before visiting Santa in the mall.

Aidan could be trusted to keep a secret. He hadn't told anyone about the time that Maddie dropped a pair of their mother's earrings down the bathroom sink—though their mother eventually figured it out on her own—and he wouldn't tell anyone about Santa's stash of presents, as long as Santa was honest with him.

Honesty is the best policy, was what his teacher back in Texas always used to say.

The truth was, seeing the presents alone would have only kept his mind occupied for a little while under normal circumstances.

He would assume that there was some grownup reason for it that he was too young to understand, and he would move on.

The trouble this time was that his parents seemed upset when he raised the question. They weren't angry, but they were eager to move on. They didn't want to talk to him about Santa, and later that same night, he heard his mother say that she was *scared*.

What was there to be scared about? Why would they be scared to talk about Santa? More importantly, why had he never thought to ask questions about the guy who could see him while he was sleeping and knew when he was awake?

Under the circumstances, he was really beginning to wonder what Santa's deal was.

As they walked up to the door which led into one of the stores at the mall, Aidan turned and saw Santa. He was standing on the other side of the parking lot, holding a cardboard sign that Aidan couldn't read, while ringing a bell.

Aidan's heart skipped a beat when he saw the man himself. He couldn't help but get excited, having spent so many years looking up to Santa as not only the bringer of gifts, but a role model for the career that Aidan once wanted to have when he grew up.

His father had since explained that only one man could be Santa, so Aidan was forced to give up on that dream.

Turning his attention back to the path in front of him, Aidan saw that his Grandma was already in the store and she was walking fast. Unlike his mother, Grandma seemed to know just what she wanted and just where to go to find it. She didn't waste time looking at everything in the store, feeling every piece of clothing to see how soft it was and checking each price tag to see how expensive.

Grandma walked through the store, right to the kitchen supplies. Once there, she began browsing.

Maddie didn't wander very far from Grandma, but she made her way to some of the oven mitts and felt their material. "This is cute," she said as she rubbed one of the mitts on her cheek, mimicking what she had seen her mother do a hundred times before.

"I had a bit of an accident," Grandma said, looking down to Aidan. "A few weeks back, I put one of my cookie sheets in the dishwasher when I wasn't supposed to and it came out all funny looking."

She made a funny face when she said the words *funny looking*, which made Aidan smile.

"You don't like malls, do you?" she asked him.

Aidan shrugged. He didn't hate malls. He just preferred the toys and video games to the baking supplies and bedspreads.

Grandma grabbed a cookie sheet off of the shelf and looked it over. She held it out to Aidan and said, "How does this one look to you?"

Aidan shrugged again. He said, "Okay, I guess."

"Nonstick. That's good... but I couldn't use any metal spatulas on it. That's not so good."

Grandma grabbed another cookie sheet. This one looked like its paint was crackling. She held it out to Aidan just as Maddie rejoined them.

"What do you think?" Grandma asked.

Maddie felt the cookie sheet and said, "This is cute."

"It looks broken," Aidan argued.

"It does not. It's pretty," Maddie said back, in a snarky tone.

"No need to argue. I'm sure there's one that we can all agree on," Grandma told them, picking up another cookie sheet.

This time, when Grandma held out the cookie sheet, Aidan looked it over very carefully. He studied its color, which seemed shiny enough. He felt it, though this didn't tell him very much. Then, after careful consideration of all these things which he wasn't really sure of, he looked to Grandma and said, "I like this one."

"I like this one too," Maddie agreed, with a nod.

"Then this is the one we'll get," Grandma told them, reading the label on the cookie sheet. "Plus, it's dishwasher safe. That helps."

Grandma made the funny face again, just before walking toward the counter to check out. Aidan and Maddie looked at each other and smiled as they followed.

Once at the register, Grandma began the process of checking out. As she did this, and Maddie looked over the small boxes of chocolate which were placed next to the register, Aidan turned and looked around the store.

From where he was standing, Aidan could see all the way through the store, into the mall. As the crowd of people shifted, Aidan was able to see more and more. He could see Christmas decorations, taller than he was. He could see a festive train, carrying kids in circles around a big gingerbread house.

He saw what he thought to be a teenage girl in a green skirt and a funny hat, but the more he studied her, the less she looked like a teenage girl. Her shoes were not the shoes of a normal person. They were elf shoes. Her hat was an elf hat.

It took him a moment more than it probably should have, but Aidan came to realize that this was not a teenage girl at all. He was looking at an elf.

The crowd continued to move, and Aidan soon saw who was sitting in front of the gingerbread house. This was the reason for the big crowd of people.

Santa Claus.

A line of children were waiting to sit on his lap and tell him what they wanted. Parents were waiting to take pictures. Elves were helping to keep the crowd in line.

Aidan's mouth fell open. He couldn't help but stare at Santa, who was sitting in a large, fancy chair as he listened to each kid pass on their wishes. He couldn't see Aidan, because Aidan was too far away and Santa had more important things to do than look around the mall for one kid, but Aidan could see him—Just like he saw Santa standing outside, only moments earlier.

Aidan's mouth closed and his reaction changed from wonder to confusion. If Santa was outside, carrying a cardboard sign, how could he also be inside, listening to kids recite their Christmas lists?

Grandma finished paying for her cookie sheet and walked to Aidan's side. As Maddie followed her and looked to see what Aidan was staring at, she screamed, "Santa!"

"Oh," Grandma said. The expression on her face was not wonder or amazement at all. Grandma did not seem happy that the kids had seen Santa.

"Can we go?" Maddie asked. "Please? Please?"

"Oh, sweetie," Grandma said, still looking less than happy. "Your parents really wanted to go and see Santa with you. Wouldn't that be better?"

"But he's right there!" Maddie yelled. "Please, please, please, please, pleeeeeeease?"

"We can't right now. I promise, you will see Santa. You'll just have to wait until your Mommy and Daddy take you," Grandma told Maddie, leading her toward the exit.

Maddie began crying, and screaming "I want to see Santa!"

People in the store turned and looked at her, but none of them seemed upset. The adults looked at Aidan's Grandma, but they didn't seem to be mad about the screaming child. Some smiled. Others looked sad and shook their heads.

Aidan walked behind his Grandma as they left the store, watching everyone react to Maddie's screams. Grandma didn't know what to do about Maddie. She hadn't been out with her enough to know that crying and screaming were not uncommon for Maddie.

As they reached the sidewalk and prepared to walk back to the car, Aidan went to Maddie's side and took her hand. He said, "Hey Maddie, it's okay. We're going to meet Santa later."

Maddie didn't stop crying. She didn't pay Aidan any attention at all.

"I hate Grandma!" Maddie screamed through her sobs.

Grandma looked hurt by those words, so Aidan looked up at her and said, "Don't worry. She says that about everyone."

"I do not!" Maddie screamed.

"Do too," Aidan shot back.

"I do not say that to everyone!"

"Yes you do. You told the mailman that you hated him once."

Maddie stopped sobbing and smiled, "I did not."

"You told a horse that you hated him once," Aidan continued.

Maddie started laughing now, though her eyes were still red and puffy and her cheeks were still wet with tears.

"I did not," Maddie argued playfully.

"You told a... cookie that you hated it once," Aidan pressed.

To Maddie, this was now a game. She said, "Did not."

"You told a car once."

"Did not."

"A helicopter."

"Did not."

"Umm..." Aidan said, struggling to think of something else.

"A monkey," Maddie helped.

"You told a monkey once," Aidan allowed.

"Did not!"

Both kids laughed now, as Grandma watched. She smiled at Aidan and put her hand on his head as she said, "You're like a little girl whisperer."

Aidan laughed for a moment and then said, "A what?"

"A little girl whisp—never mind. You're a very good big brother," Grandma told him as she led the way through the parking lot, toward the car.

As Aidan walked, he held Maddie's hand and made sure that she didn't run into traffic. He didn't want her getting hit by any cars or taken by the strange ninja assassins that his father was always telling him about.

He kept an eye out for any cars that might be coming his way. As he did this, he turned and looked across the parking lot. At the far end, he once again saw Santa, still holding the cardboard sign and ringing a bell.

Chapter Eight

Aidan's cousin, Sarah, was older than him. She was old enough to avoid being forced to play with the rest of the kids, which—to Aidan—meant that she might as well have been a fully grown adult.

Sarah was in the sixth grade. She had access to knowledge which Aidan could not even imagine, and she never let him forget it.

Two days after Aidan's trip to the mall with Grandma, he and Maddie were dropped off at their aunt and uncle's house so that they could play while their parents went off to take care of other important business.

Uncle Mike was fixing a leak in the roof, though Aunt Jessica was sure that he would fall and break his neck. She wanted to call a professional roof repairman. Uncle Mike would hear nothing of it.

Aidan hoped that his uncle would be proven right in this argument, if only because his being proven wrong would mean that his neck would be broken and Aidan imagined that it would probably still hurt on Christmas. Who wanted to have a broken neck on Christmas?

While she waited for Uncle Mike to fall off of the roof, Aunt Jessica was cleaning the house and getting it ready for a Christmas party. According to Sarah, this meant that her parents would have all of their friends over and they would sing Christmas songs really loudly, preventing her from falling asleep, even though she wasn't allowed to join the party. She thought that was so unfair.

Aidan's parents had never had a Christmas party—at least, not that he could remember. Instead, their Christmas seasons had always been very quiet. Their small family would gather and watch Christmas movies and make Christmas cookies. They would sing songs and play games. Then, on Christmas Eve, both of his parents would sit him down and read him stories about Santa Claus and Jesus—though Aidan had never been quite sure how Jesus fit into the story of Christmas.

He was curious to see what one of these Christmas parties would be like, but he knew that his parents would probably be too busy talking to their friends to read any Christmas stories or bake cookies. He kinda liked things the way he had always done them. He was barely seeing enough of his parents as it was. They always seemed to be out, leaving Aidan and his sister with Grandma or his aunt and uncle.

This visit to his aunt and uncle's house was different. Aidan didn't want to play with toys or run around, because he didn't want to get yelled at by his aunt. He *really* didn't want to play hide and seek, or go near that closet under the stairs.

Instead, Aidan talked his sister and Max into playing games in his uncle's den. Both of the other kids seemed happy enough to do what he wanted and didn't even put up a fight. This was the benefit of being the oldest in their group. As long as Sarah wasn't around, Aidan was the boss.

They started out with a puzzle. It was one of Max's puzzles, which Aidan didn't find very difficult to put together. After that, Aidan tried playing a game of *Candyland* with his cousin and his sister, but Maddie didn't seem interested in following the rules of the game. She would move her piece all around the board, and the more Aidan told her to stop, the more she tried to annoy him. She laughed as he got upset.

If he had been at his own home—wherever that was anymore —Aidan would have screamed at Maddie or possibly smacked her. She would have screamed and cried, and Aidan would have gotten into trouble. Still, he would have had the pleasure of smacking his sister.

Being in someone else's house, he didn't yell at her or hit her. His parents had always told him to be on his best behavior when he was in someone else's house, because if he broke something, they could call the police and he would be taken away and would never see his family again.

Of course, Aidan was old enough to know that they were teasing him. Odds were, even if the police did take him away, he wouldn't spend more than a few months in jail. He learned this by listening to his parents scream at the radio, when a rap star got out of jail after only one year. Aidan assumed that the rappist guy must have done something really bad if his parents were that upset.

If someone that bad would get out of jail after only one year, surely Aidan wouldn't be sent away for the rest of his life. Still, the prospect of a few months in jail didn't sound good to him. So, rather than get into a big fight with Maddie, Aidan huffed out of the room and quietly vented his anger in the family room, by punching a pillow.

"You break it, you bought it," Sarah said as she walked into the room behind him and fell into a chair.

Aidan was confused. He asked her, "What?"

"The pillow. If you break it, you have to buy it. House rules," Sarah explained. "It's a really expensive pillow too. It's made of some expensive material."

"Whoa," Aidan whispered to himself, having narrowly avoided time in the slammer.

"Now, go away. I have grownup shows to watch for school," Sarah ordered, picking up the remote control and turning on the TV.

Sarah flipped through the menu on the DVR and found a show which was recorded. She pressed *play* just as Aidan was turning to walk out of the room.

"*Christmas*," came a voice on the TV, stopping Aidan in his tracks. "It's a holiday celebrated by millions of people around the world. But, what is the true origin of this holiday? Join us as we discover the secret history of Christmas, and its most famous mascot, Santa Claus..."

Aidan turned around and looked at the TV just in time to see images of Christmas trees and old drawings of a bearded man with a pipe, who only looked slightly like Santa Claus.

"What is this?" Aidan asked Sarah.

Sarah sighed and paused her show. She said nothing as she waited for Aidan to leave.

"You get to write about Christmas for school?" Aidan asked.

"I'm writing a report for my history class. I call it, '*Lies*.'" Sarah said with a smile. "It's all about the lies that they tell us about history and religion and all of that stuff."

"What does that have to do with Christmas?"

"Christmas is the season of lies," Sarah told him. "In fact, that might be a better title for my paper."

Aidan stepped closer to Sarah and asked, "What do you mean?"

"You probably don't want me to tell you."

"Yes I do."

"I'll get in trouble."

"No you won't. I won't tell anyone. I promise."

Sarah took a deep breath and looked around to see if they were alone. Then, she motioned for Aidan to get a little closer so that she could lower her voice. Once he was standing next to her, Sarah started.

"You know how they tell us that Christmas is Jesus' birthday?" Sarah asked.

Aidan nodded, as though he had known that all along. In truth, he'd heard mumblings about Jesus, but those stories always seemed to get buried beneath the piles of stories about Santa, reindeer and snowmen.

Sarah continued, "Total lie. Jesus wasn't even born in December. He was born in the spring, or something."

Aidan's eyes widened, though honestly, he didn't see how that fact would alter his celebration of Christmas at all.

"And the biggest lie of all—the thing that nobody wants you to know—is that Christmas isn't even a Christian holiday. It's a pagan holiday."

"What's a pagan?"

"They're like witches."

This time, Aidan was truly shocked. He had heard of witches before, but only in stories and around Halloween. He never would have associated them with Christmas.

Through his shock, Aidan managed to ask the biggest question on his mind, "What about Santa?"

Sarah smiled and waved a hand through the air, brushing off the topic as though it was nothing. She said, "Oh, Santa's real."

Aidan breathed a sigh of relief.

"Except, he died. Like, hundreds of years ago…"

"Sarah!" came the angry voice of Uncle Mike from behind Aidan.

Sarah's face immediately dropped as she looked past Aidan to her father. She whispered under her breath, "I knew you'd get me in trouble."

"Upstairs. Now!" Uncle Mike yelled, and Sarah ran up the stairs as quickly as she could.

Aidan turned and saw his uncle. Uncle Mike seemed upset, though he didn't yell at Aidan. Instead, he looked at Aidan as though he didn't know quite what to say. In a way, Uncle Mike looked scared. This only made Aidan more uncomfortable than he already was.

Uncle Mike walked to Aidan and knelt on one knee so that he could be face to face with the boy. He asked, "What did she tell you, buddy?"

Aidan was scared of what might happen to Sarah if he answered. Instead, he shook his head and shrugged.

"Do you need to talk?" Uncle Mike asked.

"No, sir," Aidan replied.

Uncle Mike nodded and said, "Sounds good to me. Go play."

Chapter Nine

Aidan's father picked him and Maddie up from his aunt and uncle's house later that afternoon. When his father first walked into the house, he seemed tired. He was stretching his back and rubbing his arms as though he had been working hard. Aidan just assumed that he had been unpacking more of their boxes, but his father never told him where he had been on any given day.

Uncle Mike hurried to grab Aidan's father as soon as he arrived, and walked him into the den. He closed the door behind them.

Aidan could just imagine what Uncle Mike was saying. He knew that when the door opened and his father walked out of the den, he would be in trouble. He wasn't sure what he had done wrong, but Uncle Mike hadn't been able to sit in the same room with him ever since Sarah told him the truth about Christmas.

Witches.

He couldn't believe what he had heard, but things were starting to make sense. Grandma had said something about Santa being magical. His own father had mentioned a magic bag. Now, Aidan was beginning to question everything he had ever known about Santa Claus. After all, how trustworthy could a witch really be?

The presents in the closet were still a mystery. Aidan had wondered about Santa visiting every house in the world on one night, but if he was a witch, maybe that explained it.

Aidan watched the door to the den and waited for his father to walk out. He could hear Maddie laughing in another room.

Somewhere in the house, Max yelled, "Hey, stop it!"

Aidan didn't take his eyes off of the door. He barely allowed himself to blink. He wanted to run and hide, so that he could avoid punishment. At the same time, he wanted his father to come out of that room and tell him what he had done. He wanted answers.

The door opened. Uncle Mike stood in the doorway and looked to where Aidan was standing. He smiled, but it wasn't a normal smile. It made Aidan even more nervous than before.

As Uncle Mike stepped aside, Aidan's father walked out of the room. He stopped right in front of Aidan and bent down so that he could be at eye level with his son.

"Hey, buddy," his father said, smiling warmly.

Aidan felt a little bit better as he said, "Hey."

"Uncle Mike tells me that you were talking to Sarah today. Do you want to tell me what you were talking about?"

Aidan shook his head—partly because he was afraid to answer and partly because he really didn't entirely know what they were talking about.

"It's okay. You're not in trouble," his father said. "I just want to make sure that she didn't say anything that upset you."

"She said that Jesus was born in the spring," Aidan told his father, unsure of which part of this story would get him into trouble.

"Okay," his father said, looking down to the floor before looking back to Aidan. "What else did she tell you?"

Aidan shrugged.

"Did she say anything about Santa?"

Aidan shrugged again.

"You can tell me. It's okay."

"She said... She said that Santa was a witch," Aidan told his father, expecting punishment, but none came.

Aidan's father stared at him for a moment, saying nothing else. He then smiled and said, "She said he's a witch?"

Aidan nodded. His father seemed so relieved that Aidan didn't feel a need to go on with the story. There were parts that he was leaving out, but this was the part that he really wanted answers to.

"Is he a witch?" Aidan asked.

"Santa's not a witch," his father told him.

"But, Grandma said that Santa's magic. And you said that he had a magic bag. And witches are magic," Aidan blurted so fast that he barely knew what he was saying.

"Santa is not a witch. Okay?"

"But, how does he get to everyone's house then? And you said that he had a magic bag, but—"

"Aidan, listen," his father said before stopping to think. He took a few moments before saying, "I can't answer all of your questions. I can't tell you everything you want to know. But I can promise you that Santa Claus is not a witch. He is magical and he does the things he does because he's more than any normal person. He is the spirit of Christmas. He's the spirit of giving and caring. He inspires us. That spirit gets inside of us and it makes people look at the world differently. It makes us do the things that we wouldn't normally do for others. That's what Santa Claus is. Definitely not a witch."

Aidan stepped back and looked his father squarely in the eyes. He nodded and said, "Okay, Dad."

Aidan's father smiled once again and then stood up. He said, "Okay, let's get your sister and go home."

As his father walked away, Aidan stood still. He watched his father, thinking about what he had just said. Somehow, Aidan got the impression that his father was keeping something from him. The way he avoided answering questions seemed like he knew the answers, but didn't want to tell Aidan.

More than that, if Santa was keeping toys in peoples' houses, surely the adults would have to know about them; which meant that they knew more about Santa than they were telling Aidan.

Aidan knew that his father would never lie to him. He trusted his father to do what he thought was right, so he must have thought that Aidan was too young to know the truth. If that was the case, the truth had to be something big.

Santa Claus might not have been a witch, but there was more to the story and Aidan planned on figuring out what that secret was.

As he waited for his father to come back with Maddie, Aidan turned his eyes toward the den. There, he saw his uncle, still standing where he had been the entire time. If Aidan's father knew the truth about Santa, then Uncle Mike would too.

Aidan wondered if his uncle believed that Aidan had moved on, as he had allowed his father to believe. Aidan didn't know Uncle

Mike very well. He couldn't be sure whether or not Uncle Mike would tell Santa that Aidan had been asking questions.

As Aidan walked out of his aunt and uncle's house that evening, he couldn't help but notice that Sarah was nowhere to be seen. In fact, he hadn't seen her at all since her father sent her upstairs.

Chapter Ten

The next morning, Aidan awoke to the smell of pancakes cooking in the kitchen downstairs. It was Christmas Eve.

As he sat in bed and took in that smell, he looked out the window. No matter how many times he awoke to the sight of snow outside, it would never get old.

He got out of bed and stepped closer to the window, squinting as the brightness of the snow strained his eyes. There was something about the world when covered with snow that Aidan couldn't quite put his finger on, but he loved it. He loved seeing people bundled up and shoveling the sidewalk. He loved seeing the streets covered in melted snow and tire tracks. He loved looking at a dark object and seeing white snowflakes passing by.

He pressed his hand against the glass and felt a small part of the chill that existed just beyond his window. When he took his hand away from the glass, its outline remained.

Santa is a witch!

The memory of the previous day's events came rushing over him like a tidal wave. He closed his eyes and wished that they would go away, but he couldn't make them. They played out in his memory, revealing that Santa wasn't really a witch after all, but something was definitely wrong.

There was a knock on his bedroom door. Grandma poked her head in and said, "Your mother's making pancakes in the kitchen. You should hurry up and get downstairs before they're cold."

"I'm coming," he replied, walking toward the door.

Grandma stepped into the room and looked Aidan over. She asked, "Are you feeling okay? You look a little sick."

"I'm okay. I just have a lot on my mind lately," Aidan told her.

"Ah," Grandma nodded. "Trouble at work?"

"No."

"Trouble with the little lady?"

Aidan winced and said, "Eew. No way."

"I love that you're still so young," Grandma smiled. "So, what's up?"

Aidan wondered whether or not he should ask her. He wanted to just blurt it out and be done with it, but he doubted that she would tell him the truth. For some reason, the adults couldn't tell him what was happening. His mother had even mentioned that she was *scared* when she didn't know he was listening. His parents had seemed downright sad every time the name *Santa Claus* was mentioned.

He decided not to ask Grandma what was happening. He needed to figure it out on his own, but he wasn't sure how.

Instead of telling her anything, Aidan simply shrugged.

Grandma nodded, "Well, okay then. You tell me when you're ready."

She looked like she was about to walk away, but she stopped herself and looked back to Aidan. She thought for a moment and then said, "You know, you can talk to me or your parents about anything. It may not always seem that way, but it's true. You're going through a lot right now and it's okay if you miss your old house or your friends. Nobody will be mad at you."

Aidan suddenly remembered his old home and his old friends. He hadn't thought of them in a long time.

"I like New Jersey," Aidan smiled. "The pizza's ridiculous."

Grandma laughed and waved to Aidan as she walked out of the room. Once she was gone, Aidan's smile faded and he turned back to the window.

Outside, the snow was falling and friends were calling *yoo-hoo*.

∞

Breakfast wasn't just normal, everyday pancakes. Aidan's mother made chocolate chip pancakes, with whipped cream and sprinkles. Aidan had rarely seen her make these, mostly due to the fact that they always made Maddie hyper, which led to screaming and crying.

As Aidan ate his breakfast, his mother seemed happy. She was humming Christmas songs and smiling. He couldn't remember the last time she didn't look sad about something.

"We're going to have a good day today," she told him. "I was thinking that we might go skating down at the park."

"I don't know how to skate," Aidan reminded her.

"Me neither!" Maddie yelled, already starting to show signs of a sugar high. "Skate! Skate! Chahhh! On the ice! La-la-la!"

Maddie grabbed a handful of pancakes and shoved them in her mouth, laughing as she did it. Her mother quickly rushed to her with a napkin and started wiping down her face.

"Maddie, stop it," her mother insisted. "We're having a good day. I don't want to yell, okay?"

"I want to yell!" Maddie yelled. "Yellow!"

"Are we sure she's not drunk?" Grandma asked.

"Nah," Aidan's mother replied. "She's a mean drunk. Nothing like this."

"I'm a mean drunk!" Maddie yelled, as loudly as she could. "Hey! I'm a *mean* drunk!"

"Yeah, this is gonna be awesome," her mother smiled to Aidan as she put the napkins on the table.

Just then, her cell phone rang. Aidan's mother hurried across the kitchen to her phone and answered it. Aidan watched as she took the call, ignoring Grandma's struggle to get Maddie to eat her food with a fork.

"Hello?" his mother said into the phone. "Yes, this is she."

She listened for several seconds. In those seconds, Aidan could see all of the happiness that she had only moments earlier draining away.

"But, I was told that we had until the twenty-eighth to—No, I understand that, but we were told that we had until the twenty-eighth to get that in to you."

His mother turned away from the table, toward the kitchen window. She put a hand on her head and leaned on the counter. Aidan could already tell that they would not be going skating on that day.

"Is there any way that we could get an extension? The thing is, we just moved and—Right. Right. Okay... Bye."

She ended her call and put the phone on the counter, but did not turn around to face the others.

"Is everything okay?" Grandma asked her, in a soft tone.

Aidan's mother nodded, still not turning around as she said, "Yeah. I just need a minute. Can you watch them for me?"

"Sure," Grandma replied.

After Grandma said that, Aidan's mother walked out of the room. Though she tried her best to hide her face, Aidan could tell that she was crying.

Once she was gone, Grandma tapped Aidan's arm and said, "Eat your breakfast, okay?"

"Is Mom okay?" Aidan asked his Grandma.

"She will be."

"Okay!" Maddie screamed, as she threw her fork across the kitchen. "Whoa!"

"Maddie!" Aidan yelled, getting out of his chair. "How many times do you have to be told not to throw your fork?"

"Sorry!" Maddied replied. She smiled, revealing a mouth that was full of chewed-up pancakes.

Aidan looked to his Grandma and shook his head, saying, "Kids."

∞

Later that morning, Aidan's mother packed Aidan and Maddie into the car.

"Ice skating!" Maddie yelled, kicking the seat in front of her once she was strapped into her own booster seat.

"Not right now, baby," her mother replied. "We have to go to the mall right now, okay?"

"I don't want to go to the mall!" Maddie yelled back. "I want to go ice skating!"

"Maybe later, okay? We have to go to the mall first," her mother insisted.

Aidan sat in his seat, quietly listening to his mother fight with Maddie. He remained quiet as they drove, and Maddie yelled beside him. He continued to stay quiet as they got to the mall and walked inside.

Once they were in the mall, Aidan's mother walked the two children to the indoor playground. She stood with them in front of the slide, which led down to the ball pit, and said, "Listen to me. Can I leave you two here for two minutes while I go and take care of something very important?"

"I don't want to be left here!" Maddie replied. "I want to go with you, Mommy."

"I know, sweetie, but I need to go and do something so-so important. I need to talk to Santa and make sure that he got our new address, okay?"

"I want to talk to Santa!" Maddie yelled, lighting up with excitement.

"Not just yet, baby. Mommy needs to talk to Santa first, okay?"

"I want to talk to Santa!" Maddie insisted.

Her mother looked around and sighed before turning back to Maddie and saying, "You can talk to Santa after I do, okay? Mommy just really needs to talk to him first."

"I want to talk to Santa! Now!"

Aidan's mother then took a deep breath and clenched her jaw as she leaned in close and whisper-yelled, "Madison, you listen to me. I am going to talk to Santa and you will wait here with Aidan. If you're not a good girl, you will not talk to Santa at all. If you're not a good girl, Mommy will tell Santa that you've been very bad and don't deserve any presents. Got it?"

Aidan took Maddie's hand and said to his sister, "Let's go, Maddie. Let's go play on the slide. Mommy will be right back. She'll be right, right back."

"Fine," Maddie sighed, turning toward the slide.

Aidan's mother gave him a kiss on the forehead and said, "You're too good for me, kid."

Aidan just smiled and turned toward the slide.

As he followed Maddie up the ladder, Aidan turned to watch his mother go. He saw her talk to a security guard near the playground. She smiled and gave the guard a hug before walking off. Once his mother was gone, the guard turned back toward the playground and waved at Aidan. Aidan waved back.

He played with Maddie on the slide and in the ball pit for a little while, waiting for his mother to come back. Maddie was running around and going crazy, but she wasn't being too bad.

After some time, the security guard came over and smiled at the kids. He said, "You're Aidan and Madison, right?"

"Maddie," Aidan corrected.

The guard nodded and said, "Noted. I'm Todd. I knew your Daddy when he was your age. We used to play together all the time."

"You know Daddy?" Maddie asked, in awe. "You must be really, really old."

The guard nodded and said, "I am."

Maddie agreed with a nod of her own and said, "Yeah. And I'm a *mean* drunk."

The guard started laughing and looking around the area to see if anyone else was listening to their conversation. Upon seeing the guard laugh, Maddie started laughing. Aidan was not far behind them.

Maddie ran back to the ball pit and dove in. Aidan turned toward the guard and said, "I'm gonna go keep an eye on her."

"You do that. I'm over here if you need anything," the guard replied.

With a nod, Aidan hurried to catch up to his sister. He dove into the ball pit and started playing with her. He grabbed an armful of balls and dumped them on her head.

"Hey!" Maddie yelled, laughing.

She grabbed a ball and threw it at Aidan. It hit him in the stomach. In response, he grabbed two balls and threw them at her, lightly hitting her on the head.

"Hey!" Maddie yelled again, still laughing.

She grabbed two more balls and threw them at Aidan. One of them hit him. The other flew past him, and rolled across the floor of the mall.

"Oops," Maddie said, watching the ball. She then laughed.

"Stay here," Aidan warned her. "If you don't stay here, Mommy will tell Santa not to bring you anything."

"No!" Maddie said. "I'll stay. I'll stay!"

Once Maddie was secure, Aidan left the ball pit and followed the ball that had escaped. He didn't have to go very far before picking up the ball and turning to take it back to the pit. As he did this, Aidan could see down a long hallway that led away from all of the stores in the mall, toward an area of the mall where customers never went.

Down this long hallway, Aidan saw his mother talking to Santa. She seemed very upset, waving her hands in the air and shaking her head.

Santa seemed equally upset, but Aidan couldn't see his face well enough to tell what he was saying.

As his mother turned and noticed Aidan, Aidan quickly turned away and rushed back toward the ball pit.

He joined Maddie, who continued to play all around him. She climbed up the slide and slid down it. She played in the ball pit. She climbed the jungle gym and had a great time.

Aidan just watched, wondering what his mother could have been so worked up about. This Santa guy was really starting to upset him.

∞

After their mother returned, she sat with Aidan and Maddie near the indoor playground for a little while. She watched them play and when they were done, she gave each of them a big hug.

"Can we see Santa now?" Maddie asked.

"I don't know, baby," her mother replied. "Wouldn't you rather go skating? The line over there is really long."

"I want Santa!" Maddie yelled.

Aidan's mother looked over at him and sighed. She said, "I guess we're going to see Santa."

Aidan sighed.

"You don't look very happy about seeing Santa. Are you okay?" she asked him.

"Yeah. I'm okay, Mom."

"Are you sure?"

"Yeah."

"Okay. You let me know if you don't feel good."

"I will."

His mother held Maddie's hand as they walked through the mall, toward the gingerbread house and Santa's chair. By the time they got there, Santa was back in his chair and the elves were helping little kids onto Santa's lap.

They got to the back of the line and stood there, waiting. Christmas music was playing through nearby speakers. The elves were smiling and having fun, while handing out candy canes to some of the children.

"The line is really long," Aidan's mother said to Maddie once again.

"Santa!"

"Okay," her mother replied. "Fine. You can see Santa."

Aidan watched as his mother looked toward Santa and he looked back. She shrugged at him. She did not seem happy about the idea of her children meeting the man, and Aidan wasn't looking forward to it either. He wanted to get up there and ask Santa what was going on, right to his face. But if he did that, he might get into trouble. Even worse, his *parents* might get into trouble.

Aidan decided to play it cool. He would go and meet Santa, just to get a feel for the man. He would be polite, but he didn't trust Santa, so he wouldn't ask him for anything that he *really* wanted.

They waited for what seemed like forever. Maddie went through different phases of boredom, impatience and excitement. The cycle managed to repeat several times before they finally made it to the front of the line.

An elf came up to Aidan and Maddie and asked, "Would you like to see Santa now?"

"Yes!" Maddie squealed, rushing toward Santa and hopping up onto his lap.

"Okay then. I guess she goes first," the elf said to Aidan and his mother as they walked.

By the time Aidan reached Santa, Maddie was already halfway through her Christmas list, which now included a remote-controlled boat and a lava lamp. She was in such a hurry to get her list out that she barely looked at Santa as she spoke. Instead, she looked at her fingers and counted off each item.

When she was done, Santa replied in a deep voice, "Well, you've been a very good girl this year, Maddie."

Maddie turned to her mother with amazement in her eyes and said, "He knows my name!"

"Of course I do. You are one of my favorite people in the whole wide world. So you continue being good, okay?" Santa said.

Maddie nodded her head and said, "Thank you, Santa. I love you."

"I love you too, Maddie," Santa told her.

Maddie hopped off of Santa's lap and stood by her mother and Aidan, saying, "Aidan, he knew my name! Santa really is magic!"

"How about you, Aidan?" Santa asked. "What would you like?"

Aidan walked closer to Santa and Santa picked him up, setting Aidan on his lap.

"Umm... I want a water gun. And ice skates. And a harmonica," Aidan said, listing completely random objects that he had no desire to own at all.

"You've been very good this year too. I've been so proud of you," Santa told him.

Aidan looked up, directly into Santa's eyes. He wanted to see if they were red, like the bad guys in all of the movies that he had ever watched. He wanted to see if he could look into Santa's eyes and see him for what he truly was. And, he did.

As Aidan looked into the eyes of the jolly fat man in the red suit, he recognized the man looking back at him.

He was looking into the eyes of his own father.

Chapter Eleven

Aidan kept quiet after recognizing his father. Obviously, the situation was worse than he had ever expected. Looking back, Aidan realized that his father had tried telling him the truth the night before, without ever actually saying it. After all, Santa could see you when you were sleeping and knew when you were awake. Surely, he would know if Aidan's father tried to spill the beans.

Aidan's father had said that Santa made people do the things that they wouldn't normally do. Now it was all coming together. How did Santa manage to get to every house in the world on one night? Why were there presents stored in the closet of his aunt and uncle's house? Because, Santa was magic and he used that magic to control people.

It wasn't right. No matter how many presents Aidan got or how cheerful Santa pretended to be, he didn't like the idea of Santa forcing his parents to do things. He didn't like how scared and sad his mother looked, obviously because Santa was coming and she knew what that meant.

Aidan kept these thoughts bottled up inside as he walked away from his father, who was under Santa's control. He kept quiet in the car as he tried to figure out how it all worked and how to put an end to it. He had seen enough movies about witches to know that you had to stop them somehow. The key was in figuring out their weakness.

But, was Santa a witch? The one thing that his father was able to tell him flat-out was that Santa was not a witch. He was *magical*, but he was not a witch. So, what was he?

That night, after dinner, Grandma sat in the living room with the kids. They looked up at the Christmas tree and Grandma said, "This is the one thing that I've been able to count on ever since I was a little girl. Well, one of the two things."

"What?" Maddie asked, snuggling into a chair next to the tree.

"Christmas trees are always so beautiful. They're always so majestic," Grandma told them.

Aidan kept his eyes on the tree as he said, "What does *majestic* mean?"

Grandma leaned her head back on the couch where she and Aidan were sitting and she said, "It means... grand. It's one of the most beautiful things in the world, if you ask me."

"Me too," Aidan agreed.

"Why do we always put a star on top?" Maddie asked.

Grandma took a deep breath and told her, "It represents the star that the three wise men followed when they went to find the baby Jesus."

"Oh," Maddie nodded.

"Do you know the story of the baby Jesus?" Grandma asked, looking to Aidan.

Aidan shrugged and said, "He's God, right?"

"That's right. But Christmas is when we celebrate his birth as a human. He came to save us from all the bad things that we've done, because he loves us so much."

"Is he magic?" Maddie asked.

"No," Grandma smiled. "Jesus isn't magic. He's a miracle. He is an act of God… and, he *is* God."

Neither Maddie nor Aidan said anything. Both were confused.

"Okay, we'll get to the Trinity some other time. Right now, how about I tell you the story of Baby Jesus?" Grandma offered.

"Sarah said that he wasn't really born on Christmas," Aidan said, in a quiet, almost whispered voice. He was afraid of what Grandma would say when she heard that.

Rather than get upset, Grandma nodded and said, "Maybe. I don't know when he was born for sure. Christmas isn't about celebrating his birthday, like you and I do. It's about celebrating the *miracle* of his birth. For that, we don't need to know the exact day."

Aidan didn't answer her. Instead, he looked at the Christmas tree and allowed that answer to sink in. It made sense.

"Now see, Jesus' mother, Mary, was a young woman who was going to be married to a man named Joseph. But before they were married, an angel came down from Heaven and told Mary that she was going to give birth to a baby; the son of God."

"Jesus!" Maddie yelled, though still snuggled on the chair.

"That's right," Grandma smiled. "But Mary wasn't married yet and back in those days, having a baby when you weren't married could have been really bad. I mean *seriously* bad. But Mary didn't care about that, because this was the will of God. Now, God also sent an angel to see Joseph and the angel told Joseph all about the baby and what they would name him."

"Jesus!" Maddie yelled again, now with her eyes closed as though she might fall asleep.

Grandma nodded, "That's right. And the angel told Joseph that Jesus would save people from their sins. So, Joseph married Mary, and when she was about to give birth to Baby Jesus, they had to travel to Bethlehem for the census. It's while they were there that

Mary gave birth to Jesus; only they didn't have anywhere to sleep. There wasn't any room at the inn."

"What's an inn?" Aidan asked.

"It's kinda like a hotel," Grandma answered.

Aidan nodded, grasping the meaning much better now.

"So, Mary put Baby Jesus in a manger," Grandma continued, and then paused to say, "A manger is like... Well, it's what they put food in for animals. Only, there probably wasn't any food in there when Mary put Jesus in the manger."

Aiden nodded and said, "What's a census?"

"It's when they count all of the people who live someplace," Grandma said. She then went on and said, "And after Jesus was born, everyone in Heaven was celebrating. The angels went and told shepherds in the nearby fields all about the baby that was born and what he would do for them, and all of those shepherds went and gathered around the baby."

"There's no star in this story," Aidan reminded Grandma.

"Oh, well when Jesus was born, a star appeared to three wise men that lived very, very far away. And the three wise men followed that star, and it led them to Jesus and they gave him great gifts. That's why we put a star on the top of our tree."

"And why we get presents?" Aidan asked.

Grandma hesitated for a moment before saying, "Sure."

Aidan enjoyed listening to Grandma tell the story of the birth of Jesus. He especially liked the fact that it didn't involve Santa Claus and he didn't have to worry about that story being a part of the mystery that he was investigating.

The story brought him comfort. Just for a few moments after hearing that story, Aidan felt none of the stress that he had been under. He didn't feel scared.

Then, it came back to him. All of the clues circled through his head like sparkles in a snow globe. He sat silently with his grandmother, thinking about what Sarah had told him and what his father had said afterward. He thought about seeing his father at the mall and finding the presents under the stairs in his aunt and uncle's house. There were so many things to consider and he felt so close to figuring out what they all meant, but the answer was just beyond his reach.

He could almost hear his father's voice, telling him that Santa was the spirit of Christmas, and he had just one question in regards to that comment. Turning to his grandmother, Aidan asked, "Grandma, what's a spirit?"

"A spirit?" she repeated and then looked down at him, thinking about her answer. "It's that part of us that makes us who we are."

"What does that mean?"

"Well…" Grandma trailed off, trying to think of a proper answer. She then said, "It's sort of like a ghost. It's what's inside of us. Does that make sense?"

Aidan nodded his reply, but remained quiet as he tried to figure out what it meant.

Chapter Twelve

Santa wasn't a *witch*, he was a *ghost*!

As soon as Grandma told Aidan what a spirit was, his mind began putting all of the pieces into place. It made sense to him now, but he couldn't go to the adults with his findings. Surely, they all knew the truth and if there was anything they could do to stop Santa, they would have done it by now.

Santa didn't know that Aidan knew. At least, that's what Aidan was *hoping*. Santa had the ability to see people when they couldn't see him, so there was a chance that he was on to Aidan. There was no way to know for sure.

That night, Aidan went upstairs to bed as usual. He climbed under the covers and he stared out the window at the winter sky, trying to think up a plan. His mind was racing at a million miles per hour. Even if he wanted to go to sleep, he couldn't have.

He could hear the adults downstairs, talking and going about their routine. Surely, they were waiting for Santa to arrive.

Undoubtedly, they were scared of what would happen when he got there.

After waiting a little while, Aidan knew that if his parents were going to poke their heads in to check on him, they would have done it already. It was safe for him to get out of bed, but he had to be very quiet. If he made any noise, they would know that he was awake.

He found himself standing at the window, looking out at all of the Christmas decorations. He saw a house, two doors down and across the street, which had a nativity scene in their front lawn. His eyes locked onto that scene as he tried to think of what to do next, but as time passed, he found his eyes drifting upward toward the sky. He was looking for the star to guide him, but there were too many clouds.

He was in over his head, that much was clear. He needed help. He needed someone that he could talk to—someone that he *knew* wouldn't be corrupted by Santa. As far as he knew, there was only one person in the house that he could trust.

He quietly crept across the floor of his room, headed toward the door. Once there, he slowly turned the knob and pulled the door open, just enough to take a peek. The hallway was clear. He could see lights on downstairs, but nobody was coming.

As softly as he could, Aidan tip-toed across the upstairs hallway and found himself at Maddie's door. Slowly, he turned the knob and stepped inside. He closed the door behind him.

Maddie's room was not yet fully transformed into the princess kingdom that she would undoubtedly create over time, but it was beginning to show signs of what the future held. Her sheets and blanket were pink. Her bedposts each had purple bows tied around them. There was a nightlight on her dresser, which featured a motorized ballerina, casting its shadow onto the wall as it spun.

Aidan made his way to her bedside without being noticed. Maddie was fast asleep and even if he were to stomp his feet and clap his hands, she probably wouldn't wake up.

Once at her side, Aidan gave Maddie a nudge and whispered, "Maddie. Wake up."

There was no response.

"Maddie. Please, wake up," he repeated, nudging her once again.

Maddie began to stir. Her eyes opened, but she still seemed half asleep.

"I need to talk to you. You have to be really, *really* quiet," Aidan warned her.

Maddie shot up in her bed, eyes wide and fully awake. She smiled at him and asked, "Is it Christmas?"

"No. Not yet," Aidan answered, holding up a hand so that she wouldn't jump out of bed. "You have to be quiet, or Mommy and Daddy will come up here and they'll be really mad at us."

"Why?" Maddie whispered.

"Because I figured out the truth about Santa Claus," Aidan told her. "He's a ghost."

Maddie looked at Aidan as though he was crazy and said, "No he's not. He's Santa Claus. Ghosts are for *Halloween*."

"Do you remember what I told you about ghosts, Maddie?" Aidan asked.

"That they come into your room and watch you when you're asleep?"

"Yeah," Aidan nodded. "And who else can see you when you're sleeping and knows when you're awake?"

"Santa Claus?" Maddie replied.

After that, it took Maddie a few seconds to process what she had just said. When she did finally grasp what Aidan was getting at, her eyes widened and she took a deep breath, preparing to scream.

Aidan put his hand over her mouth, preventing the scream from getting out. When he thought it was safe to let go of her, he pulled his hand away from her mouth and said, "Remember, Maddie... You have to be quiet."

"What do we do, Aidan?" Maddie asked, still sitting in her bed with the blankets pulled over her legs.

"We have to figure out how to stop him," Aidan replied.

"But I don't want to stop him. Santa brings presents. Maybe he's a *good* ghost."

"Dad said that Santa gets inside of people and makes them do things that they don't want to do," Aidan told his sister. "That's how he gets to everyone's house. He gets inside of all the mommies and daddies in the world and they put out the presents."

"How do you know?"

"Because I found the presents at Uncle Mike's house. Santa probably put them there so that he can find them when he gets inside of Uncle Mike or Aunt Jessica. That's why Mom was so scared all the time," Aidan thought aloud, as Maddie listened.

"I don't believe you," Maddie smirked. "You're lying to me and I'm going to tell Mommy."

"I'm not lying," Aidan insisted, putting his hands on his sister's shoulders and looking her in the eyes. "When we went to the mall and sat on Santa's lap... That was Dad. I saw his eyes. That's how he knew your name."

"He knew my name because Santa is *magic*," Maddie insisted.

Aidan nodded, "Like a witch? But he's not a witch. Sarah said that the real Santa died a long time ago. That's how ghosts are made. Grandma says that ghosts are what's inside of us. Our ghosts are what make us who we are."

"I'm a ghost?" Maddie gasped, preparing to scream once again.

Aidan put his hand over her mouth until the scream passed.

"Shh! Maddie, be quiet. You have to be good, for goodness sake. Remember?"

"Or what, Aidan? What will Santa do if we're not good?"

"I don't know... But you better watch out and you better not cry, just in case."

Maddie nodded, understanding the rules that were being set by the popular Christmas song.

"How do you make a ghost go away?" Maddie asked, fighting back the urge to cry.

"I don't know," Aidan told her, as he walked to the window and looked out.

He could see the street from her window, the same as he could from his own. He could see the Christmas decorations on all of the lawns and in the houses. He could see the plastic Santa in the uppermost window across the street, lit only by the orange glow of a fake candle.

That Santa decoration seemed to stare at Aidan. It seemed to mock him.

He wondered why anyone would put Santa's face on so many decorations, when every adult had to know what was being done to them.

It was Christmas Eve. Santa would soon be coming. Aidan's mother and father would be taken over by his ghost and they would be forced to put presents under the tree, whether they wanted to or not.

Everything that had once seemed shiny and exciting to Aidan now looked cold and bitter. He didn't want presents. All he wanted was for his parents to be free of Santa's spell.

Aidan would not let Santa continue with his reign of terror. He didn't know how, but he would find a way to save his parents, no matter what the cost.

Chapter Thirteen

Aidan and Maddie sat on her bed together, trying to think of a plan. They knew that Santa could be there at any minute, but they simply did not know how to get rid of a ghost that had taken over the body of one of their parents.

Eventually, Maddie fell asleep. It was very late at night—maybe even ten o'clock. Aidan couldn't blame her for falling asleep.

He paced across her floor, trying to think of the solution to his problem. He was scared. If his parents weren't able to handle the situation, how could he?

Strangely, having Maddie in the room and knowing that she agreed with his assessment of the situation made him feel better —even if she was asleep.

Pacing made him tired. Soon, Aidan found himself sitting on Maddie's bed, just so that he could rest up a bit. Then, he was asleep as well.

∞

There was a *thud* downstairs. As soon as Aidan heard it, he was sitting up in Maddie's bed, staring at her door.

More noises suggested that someone was down there. He heard footsteps, and the creaking of the wood floors.

How long he had been asleep was a mystery to him. He was angry at himself for resting, and now that Santa was in the house, there was no time to think of a proper course of action. He needed to resolve this situation right then and there... But how?

He had to act fast. There was no time to think of a plan. He needed to go downstairs and face Santa. He needed to tell him to leave his family alone. He needed to be brave.

Aidan crawled off of Maddie's bed and inched his way toward the door, swallowing hard as he went. He was scared. His heart was pounding in his chest. His stomach was turning.

"Aidan, wait," came Maddie's whispered voice from behind him. "I want to go too."

She crawled out of her bed and walked to his side, putting her hand in his.

Aidan wanted to protect his sister. He wanted to tell her to go back to bed and to pull the covers over her face. He wanted to be a good big brother and take care of her.

He also wanted her to go with him, because he was too scared to go alone. Somehow, being the big brother and having Maddie to watch out for made him feel braver. He was older than her. He would do anything to protect her. So, as long as he was sure to put her in the same danger that he was in, he would be fine.

Together, they walked to the bedroom door. Aidan put his hand on the knob and twisted. He pulled the door open, and Maddie tightened her grip on his hand.

"I want to scream, but I'm not," Maddie told him.

"Good. Just remember not to cry either."

"I'll try, Aidan."

They walked through the upstairs hallway as quietly as possible. If Santa knew that they were coming, he might get away before they could confront him. Aidan kinda wanted that to happen, but he knew that it wouldn't fix his problem.

Step by step, they walked down the stairs. Each time a stair creaked or moaned, they stopped and held their breath, waiting for Santa to get angry and come after them.

At last, they reached the bottom of the stairs and walked toward the living room, where the Christmas tree was. Aidan swallowed hard as they got closer and closer to the room, knowing that what he would see would *look* like his mother or father, but it wouldn't *be* them. They were trapped inside, while

Santa made them do the things that they wouldn't normally want to do.

As they stood in the doorway, Aidan saw his father, looking at the Christmas tree. His back was turned to Aidan and Maddie. He didn't know they were there. He also didn't have any presents set beneath the tree yet, so Aidan knew that they had gotten there in time.

"Daddy," Maddie whispered to Aidan.

A chill shot up Aidan's spine as Maddie spoke. He knew that it was too late to undo the damage. Santa Claus—in his father's body —was turning around to see where the voice had come from. The time for action was now!

"Stop!" Aidan yelled, as he saw his father's eyes.

In the dark living room, lit only by the lights of the Christmas tree, it was hard to see his father's face. Since his father's back was to the tree, harsh shadows distorted the familiar features of their father and twisted them into something else.

Aidan could see light reflecting off of the tears in his father's eyes and running down his cheek. Obviously, he was trying to fight Santa.

"Aidan? Maddie?" came the voice of their father, but Aidan knew that it wasn't his father.

Aidan squeezed Maddie's hand tighter than ever. She said nothing. She didn't even move. She was too scared to act.

Aidan looked Santa right in the eyes and said, "Stop. I know what's going on now. I figured it out."

"You figured it out?"

"I don't want presents. Maddie doesn't either. We're tired of our mother being scared all the time! We're tired of our father being forced to be Santa in the mall! We're tired of people lying to us about Santa," Aidan said with confidence and power to his words, though tears were running down his cheek, just as much as they were his father's.

"You don't want presents?" Santa asked, using the voice of Aidan's father.

"No!" Aidan sobbed now. Beside him, Maddie was crying too.

"I want my Daddy back!" Maddie yelled.

Aidan was proud of his little sister, standing up to Santa Claus like that. Together, they had faced down the greatest threat that their family has ever known, and it seemed to be working.

Tears were streaming down their father's face now. He took a step toward them, but became weak and fell to his knees. Santa Claus seemed to leave their father's body in that moment, because Aidan and Maddie could see the pain in their father's eyes as he began to sob.

From behind the kids, their mother rushed across the living room and fell to her knees beside her husband. She was crying almost as hard as he was, but she told him over and over that it was okay.

She then looked up at Aidan and Maddie, with tears in her eyes but a smile on her lips. She said to them, "It's okay."

Maddie ran to her mother and collapsed into her arms, screaming, "I don't want Santa Claus, Mommy! I don't want presents!"

Her mother didn't say anything in response. She simply held her daughter.

Aidan took a step toward his father, but he was scared to go any farther. He didn't know for sure that Santa was gone. He didn't know how any of this ghost stuff was supposed to work.

Aidan's father pulled himself together and looked up at Aidan. His eyes were red and puffy. His mouth was twisted in pain. Aidan didn't know what to expect next.

After a moment of looking at Aidan, his father reached out. He wasn't trying to grab or hit Aidan. He was summoning Aidan to come to him.

"Dad?" Aidan muttered, still unsure.

"Aidan," his father said in response, and somehow, Aidan knew that it really was his father. He knew that Santa was gone, and that things were going to be okay.

Aidan rushed into his father's arms and squeezed his father as tightly as he could. He had won. He really won!

"I'm glad you're not Santa anymore, Dad," Aidan said into his father's ear.

"Me too, buddy," his father replied with a big smile on his face. "Me too."

Chapter Fourteen

Two months earlier, Aidan and his family lived in Texas. His mother and his father were sad all the time. They yelled at each other. They cried a lot.

In New Jersey, Aidan's grandmother sat alone in an empty house. Two of her children lived hundreds of miles away. The one that lived nearby never visited. She cried a lot.

On Christmas morning, the entire family woke up early and watched Christmas movies as the sun came up—none related to Santa Claus in any way. They ate ham and eggs. They played games.

As the day went on, they spoke on the phone to all of Aidan's aunts and uncles, and some of his cousins. They went outside and played in the snow. They took a walk through the town and tried to skate on the frozen pond. As night fell, they drove through town, looking at the Christmas decorations on all of the houses.

Maddie only screamed at the Santa Claus decorations for a little while, and then she found a way to laugh him off.

The best part of all on that Christmas day was that there were no presents. Aidan and Maddie had stopped Santa in time. Their family was safe. Their family was together. But above all, nobody was crying anymore.

Now that you've finished reading this book, please remember to post your review online!

Find Kyle Andrews Online:

www.AuthorKyleAndrews.com

facebook.com/KyleAndrewsReaders

@StarletteNovel

authorkyleandrews.wordpress.com

kyle@authorkyleandrews.com

If you enjoyed *Spirit of Christmas*,
be sure to look for these other titles:

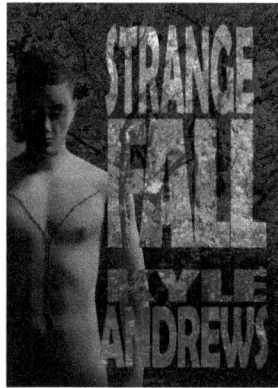

www.ingramcontent.com/pod-product-compliance
Lightning Source LLC
Chambersburg PA
CBHW060515030426

42337CB00015B/1902